SHEPHERD'S WARNING

Mervyn Linford was born in 1946 in Fleet in Hampshire. This was only due to the blitz and his earliest memories are of the bombsites in the East End of London where he lived in a prefab as a child. He moved to Basildon New Town when in 1952 when he was six years old. His address was Pitsea, Vange, Basildon, Essex. In those days Pitsea and Vange were still marshland villages and were very much his formative landscapes-cum-seascapes. As a poet, author and publisher with the not-for-profit enterprise the Littoral Press he now lives and works from home in Lavenham, Suffolk.

SHEPHERD'S WARNING

Temps et Temps

Weather Poems

Mervyn Linford

The High Window

First published in the UK in 2022 by The High Window Press
3 Grovely Close
Peatmoor
Swindon
SN5 5DN
Email: abbeygatebooks@yahoo.co.uk

The right of Mervyn Linford to be identified as the author of this work has been asserted by him in accordance with Copyright, Designs and Patent Act, 1988.
Mervyn Linford 2022
ISBN: 9781913201234

Designed and typeset in Palatino Linotype
by The High Window Press.

For my father and his silly proverbs:

one crow flying together good sign of bad weather
red sky at night shepherd's pie for breakfast

CONTENTS

Winter

Spring

Forecast

I do not write the weather it writes me:
this grey is my dull mood not just the sky
as my internal moisture and the clouds
combine as if our dew points were allied

     - were synchronised -

It seems the slanted rays of this slow sun
that skims the tide with sheens of silver light
inclines towards the rhythms of my heart
and all the stars that shimmer as they gleam
       and iridesce.

And when the midnight moment comes to pass
and seagulls like the sap in every plant
sink into the silence and the dark of my cold blood

then I like winter's reason thus defined
become the frosted thermocline of hope
that touches ice as well as summer's fire –
both phoenix and the frozen reams of bone
      that is our text.

Remember as the rainbow arcs and towers
its spectral incandescence will not last –
like us it lives its own prismatic hour
like lark song or the ghosts as breath aspires

and when our autumn corpuscles are grasped
between the mists of memory
    - and moments -
that hang their silks and glitter
when we ask and no-one answers

my inner sense of barometric pressure
responds to all the moods and millibars
that nature with its metre and its measures
condenses and precipitates like art
        in every stanza.

Summer

Shepherd's Warning

The goldfinch and the yellowhammer perch
on either side of this old switchback lane between the wheat.

July and heat are the hazy reminiscence
as I try to frame their colours each from each
    in the rose-thick hedges.

        Despite the list as red
        as the hips and haws
        of a bird-less autumn

these two between themselves and isolation
cry out their forgotten words:

"we are still here", they say, like diminished preachers
but the sermon only reaches ears of wheat
    and our deafening reason.

A Trick of the Light

Summer comes; summer goes - like birth and death:
I suppose that such cold clichés are enough
for an ode – a lament in rhyme. Breath
is inspired and exhaled and the sun
eight minutes into light delivers photons.
What can we say when leaves do all the work –
when bones and flesh and birdsongs are produced
by the death of stars – supernovae? Phones
ring, people answer. Invisible words
are pulses down a line, thoughts ensue –

meanings are deduced. I've read about physics:
about quarks, atoms, string theories, dark matter.
My horizons have no events: no tricks
up invisible sleeves. I have a hat
without rabbits - an escaped hatch in my head
where I go without keys, padlocks, straight jackets.
My gravity has never been so grave
that I couldn't laugh at what has been misread
as fact or fiction. The future is not black,
the spectrum sings, light vibrates, larksong wavers.

A Line between Us

They're only flowers some would say
these nenuphars floating on the lake
     - exotically -

Far from being English one might think, but they are
these white and enigmatic floral stars
     in the summer haze.

I'm like a Buddhist, not just Gautama's shape
as I sit here after sunrise in a state of meditation
watching my Zen-like float in a mindful way
     as I wait communion.

That message as the float just slides away
into the deep connection of a fish
when the line between what's said and understood
is as wordless and as sentient as grace
          and an open lily.

White Sunday

Baptism I forget - Confirmation I remember:
Where are the tongues of fire in my life
now that regret and age have dowsed the flames
    that I knew when young?

Now when the only whiteness is the light
that calculus has split (like we've split the atom)
      into many colours.

The birthday of The Church and mine to come
in eight hot days when Trinity has passed
and June that was known to flame is a distant fire
      that will not burn.

Veni Sancte Spiritus as the poppies flare
and Beltane's dying embers glowing red
remind me that my spirit is as bare
    as December's branches.

The ring doves speak a language of their own
that drops from the lime tree's rood like a hollow prayer
      into time's inferno.

Pelargoniums & Paranoia

There is a vividness to these pelargoniums
a redness almost mystical
glowing

      incandescent.

The way they sit against a white wall
scarlet, vermillion, claret

blood and their bruised black shadows in the sun
      like a summer wound.

Spectres of a sort, yet living still,
not in the way of plants -
of vegetation,

more fauna than flora
      ghosts of a different consciousness
            a different way of being.

They are clots in the arteries of light
corpuscular ideas watching without eyes

      - waiting -

      for what or why.

I have ripped them out of their pots
and stopped once and for all their machinations –
      their malevolence.

I shall bash their intrusive heads against the wall
and watch as their petals splatter and explode –
fall as if scattered cells from a ruptured vein
      as they stain my conscience.

An Unholy Trinity

Three types of cloud and it will rain
so say the weathermen and women
who know such things
or so they say:

cumulous, nimbostratus, cirrus
and blue in a few unbounded summer spaces
are all the clues I need for a green umbrella beside the lake.

The first large drops of rain that haunt July
and lay the dust and offer up a scent
that's sweet and wholesome

form coronets and wide concentric rings
across the surface lustre of the lake
where swallows' wings and images of sky
    will meet and fracture.

Three types of cloud as I scry the broken waters of the lake
and like the birth of something, who knows why,
the sun that sinks and rises through the clouds
becomes the golden midwife to a carp
    that slaps and sparkles.

The Church of the Holy Trinity – Long Melford

A red brick wall with capping stones
and moss and sheens of lichen
catches the early sunlight and the gloss
of the holly's burnished berries in the frost
    as it glints and glitters.

This is where Edmund Blunden often walked
and where he's buried, beneath a living rose bush
and the blush of bright November rose hips
    in the sun that never sets.

The undertones of course have said enough
of how the berries blister with the blood
      of our tomorrows

and on this stone an epitaph that states
he lives and loves all quiet things, like peace
and these November doves still unconcerned
that circulate a white unwritten verse
in blue above the chancel of this church –
      pro patria mori.

A Needless Novelty

I thought I'd seen something new
   - well, a first for me -
      a cirl bunting.

But after a search through the *Birds of Britain*
and Northwest Europe I found that they only bred
   in Devon and Cornwall.

It turned out to be instead a female yellowhammer.
At first I was upset at the lack of rarity
but then I reflected on the fact
that the commonplace
was rarely

   - let's say common -

In Barrow Hill my text is often parsed by the less exotic
and the yellowhammer writes as it reveals
its June, July and August dissertation
an analogy that's star struck
and distilled from
the sun's own
phial.

Assaying the Suffolk Stour

I remember the forget-me-nots beside the river -
the way the unseen otter was revealed by a line of bubbles

    - like pearls -

I've been scrying the glass for years
looking for something other in the mirror.

It was there all along amongst the loosestrife and the lilies –
the shoals of roach, dace, bream.

How to approach the profound when the surface glitters –
when the dream is just reflections and refractions

and up and down are deep as well as shallow
    indistinct - indeterminate.

Is that the sun's face or mine amongst the silts
and sediments - the gravel runs, the streamer weed?

Truth is the uncommon common tern, indifferent to ideas
or the swifts that skim and skitter from a hand

that we've never seen, and beauty just a casket full of scales
gold, silver, platinum, light's unfolding words - bijouterie.

Fair Weather Clouds

Green veined whites
amongst the purple loosestrife
    on a blue day.

What can I say that's not been said already
when the sun and the spectrum palette of my eyes
are stretched like the summer's canvas,
even twice, by the river's frame.

What can I say when two swans and a line of cygnets
are white and silver/grey in their double lives
        like the drifting clouds.

When the thermals climb
and the skylark's song cascades
like the weir's translucence

and the cattle graze
and amble through the grass
in their own fair weather?

Amphibious bistort
amongst the spatterdocks
on a golden afternoon.

What can I say when the glass is a clear refrain
        and the silence buzzes -

when the bees and the green veined whites
are the summer's paint and the heat -
            an artist?

The Weather Man

He often woke early - before sunrise:
neighbours would wonder why as he started
his car and drove between the fields of Suffolk
slowly - deliberately. Often a star

would hang on the cusp of dawn and daylight
with an inquisitive twinkle in its eye.
As the car progressed deer would stop and wait
as he drove on by - wondering. A strange time

to be out and about said the rookery:
Jackdaws in the manner of the liturgy
were antiphonal. A priest opens a book
in the rectory - Wisden not Donne. Words

were beginning to form - epiphanies.
He stopped by the river as usual.
Swallows and swifts were cuneiform as they dipped
to slake their thirst, or was it to peruse

the trick of light, their altered selves, like icons?
By now the sun no longer on the edge -
red and teetering, had risen and moved on
as gold contracted. It was there he pledged

so many years ago to honour Pan –
Pan and pantheist seemed appropriate.
Not prone to panic he wanted to scan
the measure of the earth, the unspoken-

ness of animals and flowers, insects
and birds, rivers and woods. Every day
he drove out before sunrise and listened.
Eventually the world began to say

what he thought he heard. It was like tongues –
Pentecostal, yet pagan. The earth's own
lingua franca, the quanta of the sun,
the inside of the seed - somehow sown

with a sacred language - translatable.
It was nearly noon, time to drive back home,
wherever home was. The rooks were waiting
and they spoke. A deer was amazed, knowing

what he knew. A priest raised his eyes, closed his book
and thought about sermons. Swallows swerved
around his house cursively. Neighbours looked
out from behind curtains and they observed

a difference - like noticing themselves.
The ring doves were syllabic and meaningful.
The small leaved lime was selfless and the world
was cumuli and blue - the sky, linguistic.

A Cold Composition

Obsessed, well, probably:
the upper sky, matt grey, a sombre page,
is underscored by clouds in long black lines
    that sing of rain.

The rooks and jackdaws, even without a stave,
orchestrate their crotchets and their quavers
on high rhapsodic wings that drift and stray
    with no direction.

Yes, I am today the sole conductor
of this cold composition as the light
    negates all music:

as summer's warm finale fades away
and autumn's voice discordant and estranged
imagines something other, even ice –
  even snow's arrangements.

Wall – August

Red admirals spread their wings as wide as light
against the warm red brick of this old wall
where buddleia upholds its purple fingers

with nectars just as sweet as this strange sight
where August still considers rising heat
  and summer lingers.

One painted lady here completes this frieze:
this mural or mosaic bathed in gold –

this smear, this slick, this glaze as clear as honey
where I am also sunstruck and absolved
   of any doubts.

No alleluias needed when we're told
without a word or reasons or the rites
  of some strange cult

that here on this old wall in pools of light
the coat of many colours that redeems
is not a dream, no technicolour sleight,
  nor wings of angels

but just the simple sentient delight
of bees that buzz and bumble when the eyes
pick out what lepidopterists describe
  with lists and language.

Lavender Walk

for Eleanor Farjeon

I remember a book of poems meant for children
and as I turn the pages, turn back time,
I recall the subtle fragrance of a walk
where lavender and bees defined the weather
and sound was the sound of summer and my mind
     was the drowse of light.

Today that subtle fragrance and the sounds
are still inclined to calm my restless thoughts
and as the sunshine strikes my neighbour's wall
and the lavender is caught in pools of gold
I turn these same old pages and the bees
as plush and pollen-heavy as they were
become that distant poem that unfolds
     like the light's proboscis.

Through Many Facets

As I watch these noonday dragonflies
that dart or hawk and hover in hot air
above the river - over the purple
loosestrife and the glare of reflective glass
that captures each rare image in a frame -
all time's diminished. These icons speak
in millions of years not moments
and where my rod redoubled now appears
amongst their sheer and timeless summer wings
my eyes, not theirs' that shine and iridesce
with many facets, fathom less and less
the clock's ideas as comfrey rings its blue
and purple bells and all is stasis.
This Sanctus kills succession as the reeds
whisper through humidity and heat
such secrets that still leave me unaware
of what it is that keeps such wings aloft
and why my sight however hard I stare
is only light refracted – never vision.

The Geometries of Time

There were shapes: squares and circles in the field
after the fairground left where the grass was pale
and the summer – passing. Gone were the shies
and the cork guns, the Teddy Boys and Rockers
on the rides, chatting up girls with fags
in their leery lips and glaring eyes
for us younger hopefuls. 'What the butler
saw' – well so did we – as we turned the handles
slowly as we scried our licentious futures.
Bearded ladies, boxing booths and ghost trains
that took us all for more than scary rides
out of ourselves and into our fantasies
on the waltzer or the chair-o-planes
flying high in the August atmosphere
till night - when the neon sparkled. And then:
the candyfloss, the ice-cream and the hotdogs
along with the clanking dodgems and the smell
of the burnt electrics; were gone, like
pennies lost in the silver slots as silver balls
dropped for the lucky few through the wire pegs
into a cup releasing a cigarette
for the secret smoker. The ducks we hooked,
the coconuts we cracked, the strange two-
headed animals we saw were just a dream,
a memory to store, no more than that
as the lorries and the trailers drove away
and the gypsies and their caravans appeared
as was the way of Craylands when the farms
required labour. Soon it would be school,
just one more year before the factory gates
would surely open and building sites
dictate with trowels and shovels what we are –
what we've become. Pale shapes of what we were

when our sure aim could knock a box of sweets
off any shelf or ring a bell when swinging
laughter's hammer. Even that field has gone:
dual carriageways and houses have replaced
the sentiments, the sights and the sensations
that Ferris wheels and cakewalks once supplied.
Now the squares and circles slowly fade,
geometries of reason, pale reflections.
The darts have flown, the envelopes are empty,
September's foolish gold has blown away
along with all the ghosts and all the trains.
The trees are almost bare, the booths are cold,
the air is chill, the geese in clanking chains
move on in straggling lines towards the marshes
and what was once the fairground of the young
becomes estranged, and old – like thoughts of winter.

Exchanges

The corn exchange is now a library:
it has its ancient columns, arches, statues –
the finials are stone-carved sheaves of wheat
        without a field

and as the cars pass by,
the juggernauts,
the bicycles,
the buses

I think about enclosure and the sheep
and then the hedge removals and the wars –
the vast intensive acres and the laws of corn and commons.

How to keep abreast of all these things
when time and tense are passing and all sense
        has gone awry.

    What is the staple now?

    Not pigs and pannage,
  not men behind the plough,
      not bread and cheese.

Small beer is all we have where larks and linnets
are as red as the absent poppies and the list
        of our misdemeanours.

Barn Owl – Liston, Essex

This bird is as white as whispers
and its flight is the air transformed:

   the substance-less –
   the rarefied expressed.

The transubstantiation
of the text that dawn delivers.

A host, the Paraclete, the weather's spirit
that floats and falls and rises on the breath
   of hope's first light.

Is this the Word with talons fully flexed
to grasp the morning's innocence – each death
   without a blessing?

The fathomless, the secretive behest
that time in its soundless wisdom tries to question –
duality's ambivalence, a prayer,
   or just a ghost?

Autumn

Wings, Wasps & Words

What are these words unwritten by the nettles –
flickerings of something understood that
      sting the mind?

These wings that worry sunlight's golden touch
    amongst the shadows –

that punctuate a grammar of ideas
unformed and yet like sap or even ink
      in spring's synopsis?

Unbalanced scales that powder my black thoughts
as they flutter like kaleidoscopic print
       from plant to plant.

And what is the denouement, think of that,
as summer's drier language talks of heat
      and light's fruition –

where each proboscis sips whatever's sweet
until the final ferment of September
when wings and words are flickerings

or hints
      of what
            it is

that autumn must remember
when nettles start to wither and the wasps
inscribe without a page or yet a footnote
the windfalls where they lie like a written speech
      that's lost its coda.

The Horn of the Light's Dilemma

Undeniable this light behind the mist –
the sun-shot intimations of the heat
    that's yet to come.

This is summer's ending:
its final fanfare –
a blast on its golden trumpet.

The embouchure is butterflies and bees
busy with the sun's last post
of nectaries and
anthers.

The pheasant's horn is rusty
like the seeds that adorn the sorrel –
is more a croak that a carefully mouthed crescendo.

Dawn is three damp valves and the sun though hidden
touches the tongue's hot brass as the collared doves
remove the weather's hat
and each note
effuses.

Robin's Pincushion

Whatever happened to Robin?
 - Robin Goodfellow, that is -

The cushion that he uses for his pins
is as rare and red-resplendent as the hips
    on this dog rose in September.

Diplolepsis rosae the wasp with the gall in question:
shall I burn this mossy emblem of our folklore –
mix the ash with honey for my sconce

    - my baldness?

Perhaps as an astringent or diuretic
it could be useful - even for toothache
        it's been said.

But most of all to place beneath one's pillow
to dream the dream of green men in the woods
or the moon beneath her midnight hood of branches
    as she beams or simpers.

Stasis & Succession

I spend much time remembering the past
because it's who I am when who I'm not is called amnesia.

We are the past accrued
and then configured
at points in time.

Without the child's stance, the teenage vision
the middle aged last chance
the indecision

     who
          would
               we be?

If every living second was brand new
without an archived reference or clue to take us back
how could we chart the labyrinthine text –
the lexicon of meanings and remarks
that made the maps we follow and digest
    like months and minutes.

And as I write this apex of a thought
    - this formed idea -

that's climbed so many steps from dark to dark
into the blue and self-reflective light of a true September

I watch the skylark hover as it sings
without a past, a future, or those things
       we call sublime.

Bright & Beautiful

All things dark and ugly - now there's a thought:
first and final causes, strange chimera
that Sunday school ignored
as the teachers taught
of love and
light.

God bless the snake, the hornet and the spider -
the stripes, the fangs, the venomous intent
that finds the wasp, the ferment and the apple
there at the core of paradise and love
      like a naked serpent.

And what of light said the earthquake and the virus
as the reaper cuts a swathe through the grain of life
as the farmer struggles on with the poorest soil
and the harvest yields but wireworms and sweat
as a just reward for his toil and his trust
      in a word – like logos.

In a Spin

I like to see the ivy in October:
the way it just denies all death and dying –

the way it climbs and coils into light
with flowers on its helices and spirals

as if all thoughts of dust were only stardust
and DNA and galaxies and time

were in themselves analogous ideas
to the vortices in my revolving mind
    and the sun's genetics.

In the Arms of a Gold October

The light and the autumn leaves express their kinship –
the way they share October's misted dream
    of a gold November.

Russet, yellow; yes, and even gold
undress as the sun in voyeuristic mode
dares to enfold the dancers in its arms
    like a wanton lover.

Each and every leaf as time disrobes
emboldened by the sun's illicit love
dissolves into the amorous suffusions
that autumn's sunlit union absolves
    from the sins of winter.

Hiatus

I am aware that autumn is upon us:
that the air is still and golden

   - that the leaves -

                 will
      follow
suit -

that swallows are not crotchets even quavers
as the summer's loud crescendo
dims and fades -

as the season on the staves of looping wires
plays a music that is quieter

   - now larghetto -

when the radials of sound are soft and silken
and each note's sustained by light and the blebs of dew.

It is rare beyond all reason in these meadows
where the river is a looking glass inclined
towards the blue and cumuli in stasis
that reflect on this hiatus and the rooks
      in their nether skies.

Il y a anguille sous roche*

On either side of the river
mist and silence, sunlight and dew,
offer a world of stillness and a truth that we rely on.

The river itself is viscous, fast and silted
as it makes its turgid way along the reach
    and around each bend.

Maelstroms, vortices, eddies:
teach us what we need to understand
        but fail to learn.

We'd sooner walk the meadows filled with peace
than look to where reflections and the deeps
are dark and out of kilter as we sleep
    through Sargasso's absence.

*There is an eel under the rock
The French equivalent to our 'there's something fishy going on'

The Drip of Water

Fog, restricted vision and the air dank –
fermenting. The light diminished, the dark
of December looming. The clock retarded.
Where is the sun and where are the stars
at night? The sun tries to reveal its gold
but fails - diurnally. It is a ghost
of its former self, jaundiced and pale –
like a host or an invalid. The pill,

taken at night by insomniacs, the sheep
tabulators - is the moon. A faint, sheer,
fuzzy tablet with a halo, a hint
of iridescence. Goddess or not? –
more like the Ice Queen - consort to the frost -
winter's king. Intimations, fictions, facts,
what is it that obscures? All Saints, All Souls:
the veil they say is thin. The moon may sail

through silks and the dripping branches, falling
leaves, but it has no answers. It appals –
nothing more. One small step for man –
war on the Romantics. All night the moon,
by day the sun, both other than they were,
revised by reason and the weather;
and here am I still mystified by moisture,
condensing air, the drip, drip, drip, like torture.

Otter versus angler – no contest:

there was undoubtedly a connection
   - a shared interest.

We eyed each other, not fondly, but respectfully.
He rolled and dived, showed his whereabouts with bubbles
then surfaced with a fish in his ravenous maws.

My float remained motionless, not a knock,
not a roach to be seen with such a visitor in attendance.

A kingfisher whistled, settled on a branch
and eyed the competition suspiciously.

An otter, a kingfisher and me:
leaves like a squall of brimstones from the limes
floated and fell and fathomed on a breeze
   that was scarce a breath.

Synchronicity that's soundless:
quartets the like of this are rarely seen
   in Liston weir pool.

Eddies and slacks, vortices and maelstroms:
the lustrous black reflections and refractions
from the silent deeps - beneath the leaves - the tessellations.

If this was a dream you wouldn't wish to wake.
Only a silver fish on the edge of sleep
could swim like the risen moon into midnight's reach -
   like a verse unwritten.

Lakeside in November

There is a sound, a sibilance that whispers by the lake
where silver birches speak with autumn leaves
    both green and golden.

A thrush believes in this
and sings its song, not once, but in reprise
as down the air larghetto, note by note,
     the season falters.

And I, as if a pilgrim on his knees,
venerate before November's shrine -
this altar that's reflected and defined
in double deeps that celebrate demise
     with holy icons.

I hear a certain susurrus - a prayer,
where leaves are strung like beads on threads of time
and light is spare and grief, somehow,
      is answered.

An evensong that's sung without those sisters
that I remember, how could I forget,
when the sun was newly risen like a host
    and the air resplendent.

And still I find the sacrament reserved
where saints and souls once sanctified and blessed
      are yet revered.

This red-distended cell that autumn yields:
that sets like a genuflection in the west –
a slow fermented sense of those far fields

when bread and wine there raised as summer's embers
offered up their heady incense and absolved
    the nightly declination
      of the stars.

Repentance, no not now, there is no need –
the mortal and the venial are dead
    - all sins forgiven -

The catechism falls across the breeze
obliquely with its golden seeds of light
and where they fall the lake receives their love -
    their humble access.

Watching –

The first real fog, moisture dripping from the trees,
that scent that mentions endings – says autumn.
Silence save the drip, drip, drip of water
and the robin's requiem. This psalter
without a psalm, no thoughts of summer
just the flicker and fall of light - leaf by leaf.

Spiders' webs dew hung, fungi overnight
fringed with humus –like a friar's tonsure.
Trees with golden shadows in the greyness
where the leaves enlighten earth, like a grate
that's just been stoked, embers, smoke, the tension
as silks vibrate to attract the light

only to shake it off when a hapless fly
is snared by this strange geometry
in time – wrapped-up in darkness. Even the sun's
diminished, undefined. An understatement,
a pallid, ghostlike, cold October eye
watching the tears roll down a virtual cheek.

- Watching.

Bull beside the River

One large black bull with yellow clips in his ears
stares across the teasels and the river
     in my unnerved direction.

The cows, heads down, are grazing
and I can hear them tear at the lush green grass
as they ruminate regardless of my presence.

What is this thing we call testosterone:
that fight or flight perception of the world
when all is calm and warm as late September
follows the swallows' wings as they travel south
     and the shadows lengthen.

The sun that slowly sets in its rags of cloud
is a red-remembered thought of all that's latent -
all those unexpressed internalised hot rages
that time has chewed and chewed but can't digest.

The bull lies down – the cows continue grazing:
teasels do what teasels always have beside the river
and as the sun goes down and the stars come out
to speak of cosmic things and evolution
I wonder why survival seems so loud
       when the night is silent.

Triumvirate

Nine white doves on a red uneven roof of crooked tiles
beneath a blue untainted autumn sky
where the Church of the Holy Trinity speaks of saints
    and our triple saviour.

A mystery that was painted in my mind
by those catechistic brushstrokes and the cane
    when I was young

and here in peace and silence and old age
those nuns of so-called mercy seal my fate
as perdition looms and the gates of heaven close
and nine white Paracletes in the name of grace
and the father and the son and the doom that waits
speak of the triple goddess and the proof
    of our strange afflictions.

Time Denuded

The robinia is only half undressed:
enough to see beyond the yellow dazzle

   - the incandescence -

a voyeur's illicit glimpse
of naked blue between the leaves.

And as the wind unhinges leaf on leaf
the striptease yet reveals more autumn flesh.

But stop, don't close your eyes, it's not a sin
to watch the year undress as skeins of geese
scribble and scrawl aloft without a pen
a less erotic story than the leaves
when the skin as white as snowflakes doesn't tease
      and all is frigid.

Audible in October

I can hear not just the wind through the autumn trees
but further off across the grazing meadows and the river

I can hear not quite a sibilance, nor yet a roar,
the weir's incessant watery loud whisper
as willows shed October's golden tears –
    the year's pyrites.

I can hear the greylags coming from afar
as down the clouded firmament like ice
the gutturals, the bars of winter's music
gather the cold notation of the stars
    and the sound of frost.

Listen: what's lost is summer and the doves –
the hollow soft syllabics of the heat,
and yet, right here, right now, in the ivy tod
a bee the size of hope, like spring's proboscis,
unfurls a thought like nectar in the throat
    of a song remembered.

The Scent of Frost

The leaves are like the leaves were
      way back then:

silver, grey and many shades of brown
fermenting where they lay in Melford Park
as once they lay and scented my lost past
      that now returns.

We cannot burn the leaves or burn the past
as long as we have minds that reminisce,
the phoenix will arise from that far pyre
      we thought extinguished.

The bridle path is always where it was
      and where it is:

as I remember frost and fallen leaves –
those poplars and the fragrance, dank yet sweet,
reminding me that time when seen askance
is not just light's successional reprise –
not brightness presupposed by all that's dark

but like today beneath these silver trees
with white-remembered flickerings that fall
and lie with all the recollected leaves
we thought to be a pall for our young grief
      when time was passing

are not at all a death while we still breathe
and yet recall what was when it still lives
      and time is timeless.

Now and then – what are they, but a scent:
a fragrance that the clock cannot defeat;
a sweet and dank remembrance of events
like a leaf that falls in stasis, in suspense –
      in a mind that's frozen.

Barn Owl before Dawn

It's not all black and white before the dawn
but mostly midnight's starless lack of colour

    until that is

a barn owl strikes a match
and light's a ghostly
slow and silent flame

that floats beside the alders and the willows
and names its contradiction ice and fire
   or feathered smoke.

Such grace in the fearful darkness where it hunts
and turns its swivelled head from side to side
as the weather stuns the moment as it breaks

the overcast inclemency of cloud
allowing light and stars, like silver talons,
to grasp the incongruity of night
  and an owl's endeavours.

Winter

Dark Bellied Brents

When I stand by the creek in Pitsea
watching the geese, the redshank and the curlew:

when the tide creeps slowly up the ooze
to where the silts and sediments intrude
between the seablite and the purslane
    time is somewhere else.

Two ends of life are somehow in this place
  - in this timeless moment -

Soon it will be high-water and in the slacks
the loud black headed gulls will take me back
(if words like back or moment still make sense)

to the same brine-laden scents and salted sounds
that wildfowl and waders represent
      to my own formation.

Vange Creek, Timberman's Creek, the Fobbing Horse:
these are where the floodplains met the land -
the low uprising hills and stands of elm.

The hawthorns where the cuckoos welcomed spring
and other things that time might understand
      like larks and linnets.

Only the elms
remind me of a truth
that disease delimits:

their absence by itself increases doubt -
the ebbing tide and the sea wrack
and the sounds of returning waders
deny all thoughts of timelessness

- hiatus -

when succession sometimes hidden like the flounders
deep in the silted moment of the ooze
remembers like the moon and all its phases

- that a backwards glance -

though in essence somehow changeless
cannot stay the starlit journeys of the geese
    or the skeins of darkness.

The Sacred Heart

Not much more than a shack,
the Church of the Sacred Heart, ersatz yet holy,
overlooking the creeks and marshes in the black
    of a bleak December.

As a child the Latin mass was far from easy,
in fact, I found it dull and lacking light
    as I dreamt and drifted.

On Christmas Eve it was different:
 Gloria in Excelsis - yes indeed!

When the gibbous moon, recumbent,
made a pact with that Christmas star
that hung in the festive sky with its sense of magic
as the creeks meandered seawards in the glow
      of refracted silver.

Three clouds, three moonlit Magi passing by
inclined my thoughts towards those flakes of snow
that fell to earth in the guise of angels' feathers
when time was somewhere else and all was cold
    and the bells were ringing.

What now as the weather changes and I'm old
Where all is kitsch, commercial and controlled
      by a different rhythm –

by a digital and hidden soulless goal that sells us what we want
when we didn't know such things were wanted.

Black Friday hangs its wishes like that star
that we once thought incarnate and a gift
          that we would die for.

The rain is at a slant, the moon obscured,
and as I walk much further from the light -
away from the glass that hung on its chain that night
      that was young and special.

The sacrament reserved, all genuflection,
behind me now as raindrops cold as ice
drill into my drunken midnight eyes
          as I stumble homewards.

Division of Thirds

There's a thin white line much further out
where the surf across a sandbank crests and falls
dividing like the brush an artist plies
the grey metallic mudflats from a sky
      of equal colour.

A few black headed gulls try to describe
the featureless and monotonal stretch of this wide canvas
by drawing curves with loud expressive cries
between the steel-like substance of the clouds
and the pools of standing water that reflect
      just one chromatic.

And still this line far out like Chinese white
defines the undefinable effect that brushstrokes
have upon the watching eye when horizons are depicted
and the frame is divided into nameless grey proportions -
when the random daubs and dashes of the gulls
explain that inexplicable domain where the palette
has no meaning and all space is singular and sightless
    as is paint without a painter.

Beyond the Bars of Midnight and the Moon

Hold on to something, not just love's old tokens:
you're on the beach and looking out to sea
and with your thoughts and the wind and waves awoken
believe in the peaks and troughs, the heart's conceits -

the oscillations. The emptiness is underneath,
or up above. Here there is an amplitude
of purpose - a form that's measured, a grief
diminished. Forget the stars, the midnight blue

expanse, the moon's white skull. Don't try to fathom
depths that are far too deep. Listen to the widgeon
as it whistles, beyond the bars that gather
skeins of geese. Look to Orion's figure

the reprise – that's winter. Hints and intimations,
choose: meteors or myths – the mind's cold limits.

Christmas Card

In the dark with the wind through palm trees by the Thames
                    - incongruously -

with the lights of Kent strung out across Grain and Sheppey
            beneath a black and starless Advent sky -

I can hear the crest and crash of falling waves
as the sift and draw of shingle down the beach
plays its discordant music,
like a psalm that has
lost its meaning.

And before the thoughts of frost and drifting snow
counter my lack of faith with their chaste ideas
    and pristine whiteness

a breach in the northern rush and gale-force riot
offers a rift of moonlight and a star
as if peace incarnate.

And in this moment's hush and the sense of calm
where a silver path is laid across the sea
like a gift that needs no gold or ships at dawn
to sail in threes from somewhere in the east

I can hear the distant gutturals of light
as geese across Leigh marshes lift as one
into the sunless mystery of night
to quell like a grail unmasked
the weather's qualms and
        my cold heart.

Note Book

A new book and a new year:
the rooks pick up my pen
and fly across the early morning fields

     indelibly.

The page is white with frost -
the rooks its punctuation.

I am lost between the margins
and the lines of receding furrows
  in a thought's caesura.

I look for a way to say just what I mean
some words between a paragraph that opens
    and then the coda

    - silence:

a theme without a theme -
the earth without a yield.

My life it seems has reached its own denouement
and as these rooks release me from this crisis
by moving off once more in cursive flight

their black and ink-like reasons, though unclear:
opaque as is the early morning ice –
refuse to stop a sentence in mid-air
   and my heart thaws.

Looking for Snow

Do we ever grow old?
I'm sitting here in my car in the dark
  looking for snow.

Do I care about the cold?
The freezing air, the clouds,
      not really.

I'm looking for snow - or am I?

Is it snow or childhood I'm after?

How many words are there for innocence?

At two degrees Celsius it's debatable -
it's mostly rain but in the heavier bursts
sleet and the occasional flake
spiralling down half-heartedly.

I'm looking for snow in the dark –
in the headlight's beams or the lamplight
nothing will escape my glance –

no sly six-sided frozen apparition
will leave the sky to melt like the weather's ghost
    when I'm on watch.

  I'm looking for snow
and even though it's raining
my cold prayer is for something colder.

Do we ever grow old
or is winter where we find what we have lost –
where the flesh, though pale and icy to the touch
detects a hint of fire in the frost?

    I'm looking
    for snow
    in the dark.

Ring Doves in the Snow

As the snow falls the ring doves rise:
the sugar beet is green, the sky is grey
and the world is wrapped in silence
        and in whiteness.

And what to say as winter's fist is tightened
and wings and weather go their different ways
        in the fading light?

And what to do when the darkness overcomes
and the clouds that part succumb to the moon's cold gaze
        and the frosted stars?

Perhaps to go
or yet perhaps
    to stay.

The ring doves find their roost and slowly settle –
the snow whips up in winds that stun and shake
and all that drifts like doubtfulness bedevils
as feathers float and snowflakes go their way
    and the landscape sparkles.

After the lull

the slow anticipation of a night devoid of stars –
the silence and the seagulls blowing white
across the black of a moonless sky
    there came the snow.

And then the wind, the lack of any respite from the cold
as wires once a whisper, barely heard,
became the voice of those Norse gods of old
    that roared and revelled.

Then what was dark, a void, a blind abyss,
became a blanched and windblown world of drifts
    and holy light.

The midnight of my soul did not exist
despite the icy reasoning of time
    and my frozen flesh.

I walked into the furrows through the hedge
enveloped in such featherings of white
that even though the season's bitter edge

requited naught but the weather's icy words
I felt as though my spirit had just fledged
    and flown away.

Winter Trees

Without their leaves they bifurcate the sky –
they make a sort of jigsaw or a frieze in black and grey.

They are the winter's answer to the light
that tries but cannot manage the reprise we know as spring.

The branches and the twigs are arms and hands
that spread their crooked fingers in the rain
to gather up the songsters, hunched and still, devoid of music.

And on this chill dishevelled winters day
        there's just a hint tight-fisted in the bud
                of something warm and waiting in the wings:

                of something blue and calm
        where March begins and April follows -
where swallows skim the greening of the meadows

and buttercups and blackbirds' bills are yellow
        and heat unfurls.

Snow Moon

Sometimes the moon is different – more deranged:
much larger as it sinks and slowly fades into the west –

a strange enormous zero, like a scream,
as dawn delivers daylight and reflects on a dream remembered.

A nightmare with a billion starlit eyes
staring out from darkness in the chill of a vast abyss.

Now as the sun uprisen from the east enlightens
the frosted morning and the trees that release their shadows –

the dream that was kissed by madness and the moon
with her crazy silver moods and her midnight lips

is warmed by the glint of gold on the wings of rooks
        that are real – like angels.

Icarus Lives

When it's still and the sun returns from darkness to the dawn:
when the shadows are as long as the days are short

and the frost is a thought that sparkles like the spring -
then warmth and the slow debacle of ideas

that thaw from their frozen purpose into song -
that hangs like a certain madness now in March

as the skylark sings and the hares in frantic circles
reverse the wrongs that were locked in the sin of ice

    - we are all absolved -

I confess that I and the moment are as one
as the sky and the earth infused with the risen host

deny all thoughts of difference as the light
lifts up my earthly wings and a flight of rooks
       into gold dissolving.

Man of Snow

I am a man of snow - no more, no less:
of course there is the carrot and the coals –
I need a face; who doesn't?

A stovepipe hat's a must - preferably in black:
a scarf and mittens for my hands –
well, let's call them twigs.

And that's enough for now:
except of course for stardust and the frost –
    I must keep cold.

The summer and the beach are not for me –
  even the spring's too hot.

I was sired by Boreas
    and the wind from
        the frozen north:

The Ice Queen was my mother –
Jack Frost my crystal twin.

You'll find me when the winter freezes hard
beneath the Plough – the glitter of Polaris.

And when the sun climbs up the dawn's blue stair
into the golden heights of an icy solstice
I much prefer the shadows and the shade
to all the gilded clamour and the glare
    of rising heat.

Touch me if you must, but please take care,
for too much love; too much of a warm embrace
will thaw my bold intensions and the air
that retains its midnight moment and my prayers
     that are cold and brittle.

Snowfall

The weather, like my mood, begins to change:
the rain has turned to sleet and then to snow
as down the weather's thermocline each flake
sidles, sifts and silently explains
     my new demeanour.

Such gifts as these that crystallise from air -
unique six-sided shillings down a chute

     - or down a stair -

minted by both memory and truth
as winter wraps its branches and its boughs
are presents without Christmas or a prayer
that the weather gives to those who find despair
     too much to take.

Each flake a virtual host that floats and flurries
or drifts across the landscapes of the mind -
a mood enhancing transubstantiation
immaculate and white without a virgin

     - without a bride -

A veil that falls and fathoms without answers
or questions of a deep religious kind.
Just ice and air in strange configurations
that takes the hand of age when love is blind
and leads the woken heart without persuasion
into the frozen forestry of time and a dream
     that's sleepless.

Icy Breath - Warm Heart

When Boreas opens his mouth and breathes loudly
    I imagine winter:

There's more than a hint of frost
and even snow on his icy breath
when St Andrew speaks of Advent
and the cold that is lit by candles.

November comes and then November goes
with golden leaves and fogs where nothing grows
    save buds and fungi

and I suppose with Christmas on my mind
and mistletoe and holly and such things
that counter time with evergreen proposals

that even the frozen prospects of the light
will not be snuffed when midnight's holy star
ignites that mythic moment from the past
    we once believed in.

December's cusp unusually repeats such lost traditions
as like a solstice dream, a yuletide fancy,
six-sidedness has crystallised on dust
to sidle down like Christmases remembered
when we were young and kissing boughs and love
    were known to sparkle.

Enough I hear you say, nostalgia's dead,
these clouds that scuff the moon
and mark the tracks
of Old Orion

                              are only air
                   condensing in the black
             of night's deep freeze -

are not the glittering Magi as they pass
towards the eastern regions of the dawn
where sailing ships by threes are coming in
across the festive tides of our unreason
                   and ideas incarnate.

But stop, don't think,
just watch these flakes that fathom
without a thought of causes or effects
or yet the need for hints or intimations

but as they are in star-struck figurations
out of the void begotten and unblessed
yet perfect and enough when all is said
about the Word when words are all that's left
             but the voice is frozen.

Gibbous & Uncertain

Beneath a tree in the country park:
a bare, and to me, unspecified winter tree –
a perfect circle of crisp and russet leaves
exhibits this strange geometry of time
    as the season passes.

There is something Euclidean here on this page of green
as the sun that sets and rises draws an arc
across December's lowered solstice schemes
    of light and darkness.

And what triangulation would I need
to fix a star on my uncertain chart
    and the word incarnate?

Frost is the only dream that I have now
as the weather loses heat by slow degrees
and the moon's imperfect zero snags a branch
and hangs for the want of answers, ill-at-ease
    in its black circumference.

Spring

Doubles in the Deeps

The cuckoo, more like a hawk in flight, than anything else
traverses its own reflection and the lake
like a hobby or a kestrel
might at speed
when after
prey.

I didn't know they called when on the wing
but as it passed above me, grey on grey,
in a sky as calm and silent as the clouds
        it rang its bell.

I know it's not a church, right here, right now,
but the lake is one vast icon so revered
        by this faithful angler

and if you think such holy thoughts unfound
in a world that's made of calculus and matter
then I'm the missing link and that's no Sanctus
that rings and rings and rings as the moment drowns
        in its mirror image.

The Colour of Eggs

A blackbird sits on the apex of my roof
and sings his springtime song
through each note's
succession.

He is the harbinger of dusk
and other things like
approaching
summer.

I can touch the mottled eggs that I remember
with a virtual thought and sentience recalled:

greenish and blue and brown, these mottled eggs
like the trunk of this tall lime tree and the sun
      through its leaves and flowers.

There are always such analogies as these
to surprise one or confound
by the way we see
and think of
time.

The song and the evening star
when the sun has set
are a scintillation

               as sound and silence
         test at the darkest brink
     the light's resolve
and the clock's

validity.

Stylites up the Pole

There's a telephone pole outside my house
and it seems that a local ring dove sees itself
    as Simeon Stylites.

He perches there for months and even years
and appears to preen his feathers and his purpose
as the females peer and circle his esteem
    as they flock to worship.

I'm not too keen on such obsessive ways
    to achieve my goals

my soul is more attuned
to sight and
surface.

I'll leave Columbiformes and other hermits
to close their eyes and parley with their god.

For me the road to heaven, my beliefs,
are on the ground beneath this holy pigeon
whose syllables religiously intoned
    are out of reach.

Instead I'll preach the greenness of the grass
and the constellated seed heads of the clocks
that dandelions leave to a child's breath
    and the death of time.

Easter Farm

Beyond the flailed hedge (the Via Dolorosa of the farm)
the winter wheat stretches towards the treeline and the sky
  with its Lenten vestments.

Purple as a warning after dawn
where the silence is the voice of those far birds
      that I remember.

"Peewit" the onetime black and white
untold dissemblance all should know
when trailing wings and wound-like innovations
saved them from their egg collecting foe
      and other dangers.

Black and white – yet blindness seems to grow with every season
and as I kneel beside this broken rail of riven branches
where I must shrive for hubris, all our sins,
the risen host, though higher, turning gold,
refuses my confession and rescinds
        all absolution.

Light-Motif

Only the sound of birds and the sound of water:
the woodpecker's hollow words from the morning copse
and the sun's uprisen language, gold and terse,
    as the dark is banished.

Only the lake's still altar and the cross that's a tree inverted:
the mallard's Lenten specula that purples –
covers the distant memory of church
    with its hidden statues.

Only the time that's vanished
       - only me -

here where the silver paten of a fish
comes to the waiting net, a recurring theme -
    or the light's enigma.

Yellow

Forsythia says something I'd forgotten:
even the white hoar frost on its yellow
petals - refuse silence. What was lost
in the winter darkness thinks of swallows
and speaks with its frozen spicules in the throat
of the dawn's blue chorus. The trees are ghosts
in their blanched and icy vestments but the doves
have their mellow notes, their own syllabics,
and love that was frosted, brittle, finds the sun
in the bones of light. All is gold and glitter
and the voice of the singing thrush. Reprise
the rich succession of its song, bitterness
denied and warmth redoubled. Days like these
refuse our frigid thoughts. The yellowness
of sunlight and the crocus, the jonquil
and the celandine's debacle that flows
like liquid gold along the ditch – like songs
remembered. The forsythia explodes
into our minds and lights a fire
in every synapse. The heat supposes
more than cold Orion. The sun is higher
now and bees and honey come to the weather's
table and the feast that the sun or son
lays out for the love of saints and even sinners
when summer's buzz is yellow and we're stung.

Λ Song Thrush & the Sun

The song thrush, like the sun, is intermittent:
sound and a brief caesura like the beams
    as they splay then vanish.

It seems that March can't quite make up its mind:
clouds or the blue that's wide and overarching
or rain and the spectral moment in an arc
        as it iridesces.

The daffodils, the embouchure of bees –
these are the things that fanfare spring's approach
    and the thoughts of summer.

    And the song thrush now
antiphonal and high in the budding trees
trumpets its own reply to the sun's hot brass
        as it blares and blazes

A Blue Day in March

Out of all that space so blue above
and green beyond the sugar beet and pasture

  - the grazing sheep -

there comes a sound that lumbers into sight:
a humming, buzz, and bumbling sudden bee
as large as one's suspension of belief
      or a fat cigar.

I flick the ash off metaphors like these
as I sip my G&T by the garden gate

  - for what was there -

this epiphany that stumbles
into the depths and nectaries of light
  with the spring on fire

will, like a puff of smoke, just disappear
as the petals from the blackthorn blow and tumble
   and the frost conspires.

Spring Equinox - Liston Mill Pool

I can hear the geese beside the river:
the gutturals of Canadas and greylags serenading
(if that's the word for such a harsh cacophony) spring
    and of course, each other.

So, this is what love is all about
- or survival if you're a goose -

this loud discordant music by the Stour
as the wind in March roars louder than crescendo
with the sun between the clouds that clash and pass
    - a brassy cymbal -

I too somewhat discordant in old age
still turn the page and play these sun-struck notes -
these equinoctial octaves that explain both night and day

and even now though love is not the same as it once was
these geese with their discordant loud refrain
as shadows fly and sunlight strikes the mill pool and my face
    finds me requited.

Vernal & Voiceless

for Rachel Carson

Can we hear again the silence of the spring?
The moon's full-rounded voice is growing thin

and the cuckoo's double-dealing rings a bell
that is muffled as the sun in elevation

finds the song thrush and the great tit less persuasive
than they once were. The omens that foretell

were once foretold but time was deaf: had ears
for other seasons, other songs, for years

defined by whispers that perplex - that leave
us dumb. Lists are all we have but even lists

are growing thin. Our golden dawns are misted
and the dusk is reddened by the grieving

of the sun, distended and diminished
as it sets on light's horizon. What sings

when the song is banished from the spheres –
when harmony is countered by discordance?

The things we miss, the sense we had of order
when skylarks hung on cadences revered

by poets and composers and the rites
of our unreason. Spring - a star-filled night

and our cold ideas - our thoughts of frost
are naught, not the death of heat as the thermals

rise and the air condenses. The wheat germ
either drowns or dies of drought and our loss

is the cuckoo's bell that will not repeat,
or the primrose, pale as pebbles in a stream

that will not flow. The notebook and the pen
are a disconnect - a taxonomy removed

from a different text that we can't remember.
Where is the light, the love, the imagined truth

that was loud before the silence held its breath -
before the spring was muted - unexpressed?

Goldfinches

These tinkling tiny cymbals in the air
are the rarest instrumental thin vibrations
that share their vernal music with the light
    and the leaves unfurling.

These finches that have risen like the sap
or the glare of the gilded sun in the deep blue sky
are like jewels or an Easter prayer or the golden palm
or the hazel catkin's red-resplendent vibes
    that my mind remembers.

Diminutive these things - these springtime thoughts
that touch like the tug of time at the heart's worn strings
but the bow that's drawn by the wings of returning swallows
still strikes a once lost chord as the goldfinch sings
    and the sound enlightens.

Buzz

The sun speaks in March
and the leaves unfurl their tongues
     in mute reply.

Loudness is not needed when the light
is as soft and seeming silent as the seeds
  with their summer music.

The buzz is about the bees and their heavy flight
as they lumber through the airwaves to alight
  on the soundless flowers.

Style, stigma, ovary and anther
repeat their yearly language that requites
the lust of the lover's lingering proboscis
    in a dust of pollen.

Heaven & Hell

I know I'm old but if I climb this tree
forgetting if I can the thought of weight and gravity

when I get to the top, beyond the bole, the boughs,
the twigs and branches, even the topmost leaves
    and the songs of birds

will I reach the sheer blue heights where angels speak
of heaven and the sight of the great unseen
    and the end of darkness

or will the branches break as I fall to earth
with a thud that wakes the underworld from sleep
    and its Orphic dreams

and will the songs sing on and never cease
because I turned and looked at the face of spring
    when my love was dying?

Symbols, signs, emblems: snowdrops perhaps

with December left behind – looking for light
and the sun's ignited candle, the match
that strikes, the wick that burns, the dykes not white
or black as we remember but sunstruck
where the harrier's on fire and the lark –
well, yes, ascendant. The bees are loud
in every golden throat and the very clouds
thought lonely in the past are the vocal chords
of songs or maybe vows that the blackbird
sings when the crocus and its bill record
this springtime hymnal and the sounds of words
unspoken. Thoughts are the wings of swallows
as they swerve across the cold ideas
of winter's snow and all that follows:
like cuckoos, swifts and Mayday winds that veer
into the south. Campion and stitchwort
in the woods where the bells that ring are fragrance
understood - however subtle. Sigils
such as these in which we trust, forget
the spider's business and its webs that tangle
our perspective and the truth. The text
we weave, the fangs we would avoid, rankle
when romantically inclined we think
of light - and even love. And yet the spring
right now is all we have – is all we know:
soon enough the dog rose and its star
will frame the cuckoo's silence when it goes
and leave us to the heat's unsought advances –
just memory and portents - intimations.

Flames & Fancies

My bird hide is my car: it's a perfect
place for jizz and a twitcher's lens – for pens

and notebooks. The hedge and trees are wrecked
by spring's harsh winds but nothing stops the wren's

loud reel and rattle – the bell the goldfinch
rings, its ting and tinkle, or yet the pink

pink, pink of every chaffinch who sings
for love – or yet survival. How bold

and brash the weather is today. The branches
bend and thrash beneath the clouds that chase

their shadows. And in the blue and grey
of this cold light - the prink and preen of chance:

a goldcrest and a blackcap catch my eye
and March, a match that's struck - becomes a fire.

Figure Skating

At minus four the river is on fire:
the mirror and the smoke are not a lie
as veils and rising columns all awry
drift across the meadows or aspire
towards the blue and sunstruck morning sky
  where thought is gilded.

The frost invites three hares
 - three dawn-lit embers -

to rake amongst the ashes of the night
as instinct or whatever, like a spark,
ignites the springtime madness of their minds
    that spit and sputter

  - and high above -

a buzzard on the ice of this blue air
circles like a skater to an eye
obsessed, not with the facts, but with the figures
that turn the river's glass and all that fumes
to more than smoke and mirrors in the light
    that burns and blazes.

Physics & Fancies

The weather brings its memories:
then or now, whenever, it's all the same.

One can feel the time and place as it touches skin
      - the sun that is -

or the wings of a singing skylark
reaching the ear of spring
with the thought
of summer.

I was there and I am here
and there is now and
here is perhaps
tomorrow.

All of this has a name - the *genius loci:*
the mirror recedes both ways
and we are there divided
as we regress *ad*
infinitum.

The skylark singing now, this quantum speck,
this particle, this wave, this oscillation,
sings its cosmic song, each lyric phrase,
      each falling cadence

                      in infinite
                unnumbered
        soundless ways
in separate places.

I wonder where I am right here, right now,
in all the many pasts and many futures
as ghosts appear like wavelengths out of phase
from worlds as coextensive as a date
          without a day.

Angles

The world is turning green, is turning yellow –
leaves and daffodils, celandine and nettles,
    winter wheat and coltsfoot.

These are the things that spring would like to mention:
the sticky buds that open and the bills
    of the singing blackbirds –

the wheezing of the greenfinch and the sun
more golden than the primrose or the breasts
        of returning wagtails.

The crocus is a fresh wide-open gape
like a nestling that is fed by the risen sun
when the swallow slakes its dry Saharan thirst
beside the kingcups doubled in the lake
        and my reflections.

How deep and green like jade is this cool water
where the rudd with golden scales are wide awake
to every hatch and insect that's beholden
to the green and yellow slow unfolding pace

that lofts the brimstone's wings and sinks my float
down to the nymphs of demoiselles and notions
of carp in the gilded cloisters of a hope
        when the bait is taken.

And up the glimmering thermocline they come
like mercury or sap and all those things
that temperature and time and gold conceits
on different scales, on different thoughts that swim

into the waiting mesh of liquid light
to thrash like a drowning man in the dash and dazzle
of sunlight and the sentience of spring
    with its fins on fire.

The Last Writes

In the end there was the Word
and the Word was death.

The final breath of dawn
was the birth of dusk
and eternal darkness.

The owl was wise enough to call all-night:
to keep its swivelled eyes amongst the stars
in case it passed from wakefulness to sleep
        and slept forever.

I grasped just what I could as daylight died
and Venus followed on behind the sun
into the black and silent midnight skies
    that were vast and mindless.

I grasped the moon's cold phases as it passed
from tide to tide insanely like an eye
that was wide and jaundiced

and when the dark ecliptic said goodbye
to lunacy and the sun's reflected gold
and the Biro's ink, expressionless and dry,
foretold no more the seasons and their rites

I closed the book as nature closed my eyes
and turned the light's denouement way down low
and there all thought, all feeling, all sensation,
slowed to the lack of tense and succession's coda –
    to the truth unspoken.